# POEMS FOR LIVING

## Theodore C. Kent, Ph.D.

### HUMAN SCIENCES CENTER PRESS

II

# DEDICATION

To Leonardo's Mother

# TABLE OF CONTENTS



**Topics covered listed below are by poem number**

INDEX OF POEM TITLES                Page 107

# ACKNOWLEDGEMENTS AND COMMENTS

My wife, Shirley, edited the book and made suggestions that helped to create its format. Pamela Duffy typed the poems on the computer, alphabetized the titles and made suggestions.  I am grateful to Ernest Cords, a computer consultant, who designed the appearance of the book and took personal responsibility for its final production.  I thank my friends who read individual poems and said that some of them helped them in coping with sorrow, gave them insights, and that some of them brought them smiles. Their responses to the poems motivated me to collect them and put them into the form of this book.

The poems were written with my whole heart and some of them with a twinkle in my eye.  Several sum up ideas that I have expressed in prose in books written earlier. Most of them were written recently but a few go back to earlier days.  Throughout the book I had one goal.  It was to help the readers of the poems feel better about themselves, cheer them up, encourage them to like themselves, and see the good and beauty that exists in the world.

# 1.  WHY I SAY IT IN POETRY

It has been said,
"Poetry is the smile on the face of truth."
But it should also be known
That it is the tear that drops from the heart

Poetry is the alchemy
That combines mind and emotion
And makes them into something larger
Than each could be alone

Poetry lifts the veil
That hides the essence of joy and sorrow
And sings to them
With all the rhythms of life

And as joy and sorrow listen
They become more beautiful.

## 2.    SHARING*

A mountain stream leaps on its way
Gurgles, hums and sighs
A solid rock stands in its flow
Silent, beneath the skies

The water swirls around the rock
Continuing on its way
Determined to move downstream
While the rock's goal is to stay

You'd think they'd fight and quarrel
But what you see instead
Is rock and stream under one sky
Sharing their river-bed

Let nature be our teacher
Respect each other's worth
And as we walk our separate paths
In peace, let's share our earth.

(P.S.  Need I give publicity
To the rock's and stream's different ethnicity?)

---------------

* Selected for inclusion in a book of poems,  <u>The Path
Not Taken</u>, The National Library Of Poetry, 1995

# 3. THE LOAN OF LIFE

Life is not a gift
It is only a loan to you
Like a library book
That must be returned

We don't own life
We belong to it only
As its servants
As life, in turn, serves all else there is

Do what you wish with things you own
But you do not own yourself
So you cannot do whatever you wish to do
With property that is not yours

You are allowed to live on earth
If you pay the rent that is due
And keep up the property
To avoid eviction

Only because you do not own yourself
Do you give life its meaning
Which is that you are owned by something
Larger than yourself

Every day ask, "When I return my life
To its Owner to be loaned to others
Will the way I am living my life
Enrich theirs?"

## 4.    IF YOU TRANSCEND

If you transcend
People can't hurt you
Since your heart
Lies beyond their reach

But your heart can reach them
If you transcend
Because you will pity them
For hating

It has been said, "Those who hate,
Know not what they do."
They know not that their lives narrow
And that yours expands with forgiving

A person who hates
Becomes hate's victim
A person who loves
Becomes a lover.


## 5.    ONLY A DROP OF HAPPINESS

If in all of your life
You've had only one drop of happiness
You've had all of the happiness in the world
Happiness has neither size nor weight
Every drop is an infinite ocean

Happiness cannot be measured
Even if its details fade
The heart and soul of happiness remains within you
So reach out with an open palm

And let a drop of happiness fall into it
Look at it now
It will draw you away from your sorrow

Lift your mind and stretch it towards the past
As if you were reaching upwards to yesterday's heaven
Let the drop of your former happiness
Grow larger and larger until you are immersed in it
Then no matter what happened today
Happiness will return to you.


## 6.   WHAT SETS HUMANS APART?

What sets humans apart
From the rest of nature?
Is it kindness?  Is it Love?
Sadly, I answer, "No."

Is it our two-legged gait?
Is it our brain's vast complexity?
Is it found in our words or language?
Wisely, I answer, "No."

These things I've mentioned
Make us different – yes
But differences need not set us apart
In nature, earthworms coexist with eagles

What really sets us apart?
It is this very question
The question, "What sets us apart?"
Sets us apart

So it isn't "higher" or "lower"
And it isn't "better" or "worse"
It's only a question that has no answer
That sets us apart.


## 7. LOVE BEAUTIFIES

They say "beauty is in the eyes
Of the beholder." They are wrong
Beauty is in the heart of the beholder
Only with your heart
Can you make things beautiful

No matter what people look like on the outside
Even the ugliest people in the world
Become beautiful if you love them
Because love penetrates deeper than the eyes can see
To discover what is really there

I am not talking of infatuation
Which is only the false love of love
False love is a siren who misleads
It is selfish and causes the heart to make mistakes

True love is mature, wise, and unselfish
It makes things beautiful with unseen power
Like a flower even after it wilts
Which your dearest one sent you
And the picture with colored scribbles
Drawn by your young grandchild

When someone who loves you
Shares your house it becomes a home
And it remains beautiful every minute of the day

Because love is there
When love leaves it becomes a house again

So, my friend, do not be misled by the words
"Beauty is in the eyes of the beholder,"
Unless behind those eyes
Beats a heart filled with love.


## 8.   HOPE

When things go wrong
A hopeful thought
Is like a flower
Swaying in a storm

Let your distress
Find its small niche
Within the larger picture
Of your total life

Like a flower
In a storm
Serenity survives
The turmoil of the moment

Your pain will ebb
When your life and you
Walk arm in arm again
On your journey

And then, believe me,
You will find a deep peace
Within yourself
You had not known before.

## 9.  THE ROAD OF YOUR LIFE

As you travel along the road of your life
You linger here and there
Sometimes you stop when you see the sign,
"This is no thoroughfare."

There are times when you pause and look around
At beautiful fields of flowers
At other times you weaken and rest
And delay your journey for hours

Once in a while you pass a sight
Which you much prefer not to see
In disbelieve you say to yourself
God never mean this to be

Your road takes you through mountains of joy
Through valleys of thorns and pain
You hurry through them as fast as you can
Grateful you don't have to remain

The remarkable thing about the road is
It was first traced out in sand
And in drawing its ups and down on the map
You, yourself, lent God a hand.


## 10.  "LOVE ONE ANOTHER"

I once met a stinging bug
That begged me for a loving hug
It said, "I am in love with you
And now I'll prove that this is true."

Because it was in love with me
It sat itself upon my knee
And said, "When humans love they sing
When bugs love they also sting!"

And now its ardent mood I matched
As furiously its sting I scratched
With lethal speed my palm descended
And that's how the bug's love ended

The tragic tale I have related
Shows love must be reciprocated
And also shows that love that sings
Is safer far than love that stings.


## 11.   BORN AGAIN

When the sunlight breaks
Over hills and lakes
And bathes the world in light

All women and men
Are born again
Regardless of their plight

It's nature's gift
To give you a lift
Every day the sun arises

In the morning mist
Be an optimist
There may be pleasant surprises!

## 12.    HE'D NEVER LEAVE HIS DESKTOP COMPUTER

He won a free trip to the South Seas
Therefore, he could afford to go there with ease
He said that he didn't really mind
Leaving his wife and children behind

With great emotion and trembling lip
He finally refused to take the trip
The reason was - could there be anything cuter?
He couldn't bear to leave his desktop computer.


## 13.    BAD THINGS HAPPEN TO GOOD PEOPLE

Bad things happen to good people
And a bad thing happened to you
Searching for reasons misleads you
All you can know is, it's true

Luck may be unkind to good people
And no one can tell you why
Some bad people go on living
While some good people suffer and die

Don't ask God to explain it
Nor put it at Satan's door
Good people will learn to accept it
And live their lives as before

Life does not promise you fairness
This has to be understood
By those who think that rewarding
Is how God repays those who are good

The things that are the most precious
Exist just in order to be
Your reward is honestly saying,
"Goodness lives within me."


## 14.  CARS THAT PASS IN THE NIGHT

A single, fragile ray
Sketching a leaf, a twig, against the dark sky
It well might be
The first faint glimmer of the morning sun
Were it not much too early

A thin, white ribbon
Searching, so it seems, for something on the road
It widens
Doesn't seem to find what it is looking for
And widens more

Two bright disks appear
A dazzling avenue of light
A glare that hurts the eyes
And suddenly it's gone and all is dark again

Who were those people in the passing car?
Had we encountered them in the days when people
Talked as they passed each other on the road
Would we have found that we were kindred souls?


## 15.  IN A NURSING HOME

A nursing home, you've heard before
Is like a jail with a locked door
It may be true but keep in mind
Other views you'll also find

Separation from those dear
With only other patients near
Leaving your own home behind
And to a nursing home confined

Makes you feel you've been forsaken
But in this you are mistaken
God's bright gift can change your mood
It is called, your attitude

Don't decide,  "This is no way!"
Say instead, "It is okay."
Don't condemn it in advance
See it as a second chance

Now that you are handicapped
Even if in bed you're strapped
Your mind still is free to soar
Unencumbered as before

Not held back by any door
From reaching a distant shore
You'll see others there impaired
And you'll find your ailments shared

You reply, "When it's not you
Hard things seem easy to do
Only those who must go through
Tragedies can have my view."

I agree, but don't forget
There are other factors yet
One can greatly change one's mood
With a different attitude

Even those with limbs defective
Can maintain a good perspective
Patients when opinions sharing
Say, "The staff is kind and caring."

Here's the message of this poem
If you're in a nursing home
Do your very best to try
To remember there's a sky

In the sky there is a star
Shining for you from afar
Every dark and lonely night
It will always be there bright

Your star isn't hard to find
You can see it in your mind
And no matter where you are
It will always be *your* star.


## 16.   FIRST ASK "WHY?"

In our world today we often ask,
"How do we do it?"
And rarely, "Why should we do it?"
We've become doers rather than thinkers

Because we mostly ask, "How can we do it?"
The world overflows with garbage
Had we first asked "Why do it?"
The world would be more beautiful

Tirelessly we try to cure the world's ills
Never stopping to ask, "Why do they exist?"
So we do this and that, and that and this
And the ills we cure are replaced by new ones

"How?" is answered by obtaining directions
"Why?" demands that we think before we act
And that is too time-consuming
In our great rush from birth to death

For "how?" we obtain instructions from people
For "why?" we must listen to God
Who wants to stop and listen to Him
When listening to ourselves is much easier?

My friends, start now to ask yourself, "Why?"
So you can contact that part of God within you
That gives life its direction
And tells us when *not* to ask, "How?"

That part of God within you will not tell you
*How* you can gain greater happiness
It will not tell you *how* you can be more successful
Instead, it will tell you not to ask God for favors
Before you answer, "*Why* do I deserve them?"


## 17.   INNER PEACE

If you are tense and troubled
And cannot find inner peace
Turn your mind's eye to an imaginary screen

On the screen see the calm water of an ocean bay
Around it tall trees stand on duty to protect you
Among the foliage there are colorful flowers
That seem to send you personal messages of love

Now let this scene enter your mind
And you will feel safe and comforted

Imagine that as you look up you see
A bird soaring across the sky
With hardly a flap of its large wings
It is a message to you that you can rise
Above your present troubles

Relax as your breath joins the whispers
Of the light breezes all around you
Feel a healing warmth as if a blanket
Were spread over you by angels' hands

Think of the smooth blue-green water of the bay
And of the bird that represents your renewed spirit
Hear the soft breezes whisper, "Peace be with you."
Listen to yourself say, "I am at peace."

In the future you can again return to this scene
And in your mind see the calm water, the bird, the trees
That lie beyond the turmoil of the present moment
Then you will find that in the world in which you live
There is more hope than you had thought there was.


## 18.   THE REWARD

If there's a job you must do
That doesn't interest you
It is likely you'll delay
Doing it, day after day

Just begin to make a start
Put your mind on that first part
If you do things one by one
All your work will soon be done

Start right now, this very minute
And put you heart and soul in it
If you do not start today
Tomorrow you'll feel the same way

Once you really have begun
Just imagine that it's fun
Like a puzzle to be solved
You may find yourself involved

After you have solved the puzzle
You will really have to hustle
To avoid being defeated
By work still uncompleted

You must test your strength of will
And continue on until
Everything is done and finished
With your will left undiminished

If you've not procrastinated
You should be congratulated
You've earned even more than this
You deserve to get a kiss!

Read this poem to someone dear
Who may happen to be near
And I honestly believe
That a kiss you will receive.


## 19.  PREFERENCE

Whales are big and very strong
Salmon can swim fast and long
Porpoises have lots of fun
But I'm glad that I'm not one

To be human is my fate
I, myself, congratulate
That it was the good Lord's wish
Not to have me born a fish

I've good reason to thank Him
Since I don't know how to swim.


## 20.   CHOICES*

Jean likes red roses, Sue prefers pink
John enjoys talking, Sam wants to think
Just as we have different voices
We also make different choices
Different voices, different choices

Helen likes coffee, Betty prefers tea
Margaret loves the mountains, Mary likes the sea
Pleasant is the music when different voices sing
Great is the diversity different choices bring
Different voices, different choices

Mrs. Jones likes dogs, Mrs. Smith likes cats
Mrs. Brown just rid her house of a lot of rats
Some people decide they want no pets at all
A few women like short men but most like them tall
Different voices, different choices

Jim likes to swim, Joe likes to run
Bill finds chess boring, Art finds it fun
Some prefer eating while other like sleeping
Most like to laugh, but a few enjoy weeping
Different voices, different choices

Some of life's decisions should be left to you
But there are some people who say that isn't true
They insist what *they* like, you must like too!
Their voices are high, and your voice is low
That should inform them of what they must know
Different voices, different choices.

---

* This poem summarizes some ideas in my book, <u>Conflict Resolution—A Study In Applied Psychophilosophy</u>, Ox Bow Press, 1986

## 21   REPENT

We all equate
Our mental state
With fate

But that's not true
If we go through
The iron gate
Of hate

It'll be too late
To blame our fate
To blame our mate
To compensate

To ever find
A peace of mind
Of any kind
Repent!

You can be sure
It is a cure
From heaven sent
Repent!

But the above
Is not enough
What's really meant
Is don't repent

Instead, live life
To avoid strife
Trade hate for love
And that is enough.

———————

P. S. One thing makes a good life easier to live,
    You don't have to *like* those you love and forgive.


## 22.   A POEM NOT TERRIFIC BUT SOPORIFIC*

I shall sleep
Sound and deep
I shall find
Peace of mind

Deep, deep, deep
I shall sleep
Deep, deep, deep
I shall sleep

I shall listen
To the rhythm

In my chest
As I rest

Deep, deep, deep
I shall sleep
Deep, deep, deep
I shall sleep

All my cares
All my scares
Fade away
With the day

Deep, deep, deep,
I shall sleep.
Deep, deep, deep
I shall sleep

I am sure
I'm secure
I don't fear
Being here

Deep, deep, deep
I shall sleep.
Deep, deep, deep
I shall sleep

No more whys
No more lies
No suggestions
And no questions

Deep, deep, deep
I shall sleep

Deep, deep, deep
I shall sleep

Now, now, now, sleep, deep, deep, deeeep........

---

* If you have trouble sleeping whisper this poem to
yourself at night.  I could hardly keep my eyes open
while writing it.


## 23.  MONEY

You cheat yourself of life's true joy
If money is your highest goal
Because by winning the money game
You risks loosing your soul

You need money to pay your bills
You need it to feel secure
But most of the ills you'll have in your life
No amount of money can cure

Some cheat, mislead, deceive and lie
In order to acquire more
They do it without trace of guilt
To become wealthier than before

No money can ever be of more worth
Than lending a helping hand
Only the good deeds you do in your life
Leave your footprints in the sand

"You can't take it with you," it has been said
Everyone knows that's true
Even when you're alive you don't own your money
If the money you've earned owns you!


## 24.   YOU DON'T HAVE TO BE FAMOUS*

You don't have to be famous
You just have to be you
Remembering that the universe
Records all things you do

All things are eternal
Nothing disappears
Your hopes, your deeds, your daydreams
Your laughter and your tears

Your deepest thoughts and secrets
Through light-years will not fade
Because they are the building blocks
Of which the world is made.

---------------

* This poem reflects ideas in Chapter Two in my book,
<u>Mapping The Human Genome—Reality, Morality, And
DEITY,</u> University Press of America, 1995.


## 25.   COPING WITH CHRONIC PAIN*

Pain is your friend
Pain tells you that there is something wrong

It does more
It tells you where the problem is

Pain is also your enemy
When he overstays his welcome
And moves in with you
As an unwanted guest

"Go back to where you belong!"
You demand of pain
I have received your message
Now leave me and go home!"

Pain does not listen
You shout in anger
"I don't need you anymore
Go back where you came from!"

Pain grins and tells you
"I love you.  I need you to live
I am nothing without you
Your house is my house now."

You run to your savior, the doctor
He promises, "We'll try to evict pain."
You say, "Eviction is too good for pain
Give him capital punishment!"

The doctor prescribes pain killers
You swallow them eagerly
Pain is shocked
"Why do you do this to me?" pain asks
"I love you."

The pills begin to work
Pain retreats and sulks
But refuses to leave you
"Something is still wrong with you," pain says
I must remain with you until it's fixed."

"It can't be fixed!" you shout at pain
"Go on your way!"
Pain pretends not to hear you
You complain to you doctor,
"The pain killer didn't kill pain."
The doctor sighs.  He's heard all this before

"I prescribed a strong pain killer," he tells you
"Your uninvited guest likes you too much
Pain wants your attention
And will never leave you
Pain thinks he owns the house in which you live."

You ask a wise poet
"What can I do to rid myself of pain?"
"There is only one way" the poet tells you
"You must move out of your home
Let pain have it."

"But that's not poetic justice!" you protest
The poet agrees and says with gentle eyes
"Tell pain that you'll rent another house
And leave the house where pain lives now."

You rent the house across the street
Pain remains in your former home
Your rented house will never let pain enter
When you are there and look across the street
Pain, reaches out for you

Pain screams, "Come back!  Come back!"
You laugh and wave "hello" to pain

Be glad that pain no longer owns you
Pain only owns your former house
That, in your mind, you have abandoned
To move into your new rented home

When you now look out of your window
You see pain at the window of your former house
Pain screams, "come back, come back, I love you!"
You throw pain a kiss from across the street.

———————

*Some people learn how to handle chronic pain by a
technique known as "imaging."  With this in mind, this
poem may make sense to those who have used this
method of pain control.  The "rented house" is their new
body-image which follows their determination not to let
chronic pain dominate their lives.

## 26.  LOVE THERAPY

When the sky is gray
And your spirit is low
You've lost your way
Don't know where to go

Your hope is gone
For joy on this earth
And your life is forlorn
And no longer has worth

You long for the end
And are ready to die
Believe me my friend
It's not time for good bye

You can find a new way
If you take an old street
That leads out of dismay
Away from defeat

It restores lost hope
And brings out the sun
If you look all around
To love someone

To be loved, takes others
Who may not be there
But *you* can love others
You find everywhere.


## 27.  GENERATION GAP?

Seniors reminisce of the "good old days"
Youngsters condemn senior's old foolish ways
And complain of the mess that young folks inherited
They insist that no thanks to the old guys is merited

However a senior says, "People were good
When we were kids in our old neighborhood"
He points out that with each passing year
There's an increase in crime, murder, and fear

Young people retort, "You old guys lacked vision
When you put our country into its present position

It's your acts not ours that caused the condition
For which you now blame us with your derision."

"You're wrong!" an oldster who heard him, maintains
"We don't carry guns - all we carry is canes
We only take our prescribed medication
While illegal street drugs abound in our nation."

A white-haired senior adds, "Please don't blame me
Just think of the violence you see on TV
It's only the young and brash generation
That imitates violence throughout our nation."

"Ho! Ho!" said a youngster, "Everyone knows
Its not the young people who sponsor those shows
It's the TV producers who pretend they are funny
For one reason only - they want to make money!"

From ancient times the theme is the same
Elders and youngsters each other blame
For causing the problems with which they must cope
And creating a world were there isn't much hope

What shall we say to the young and the old?
A long time ago the real truth was told
"Just accept the world as you find it today
And don't look around for who made it that way."

Instead of blame and harsh accusation
Lets all work together to improve our nation
Make it kinder, more peaceful, and prosperous too
For seniors like me and for youngsters like *you*.

## 28.  SUCCESS IN MARRIAGE

Said a married lady who was wise
Marriage consists of compromise
It cannot come if every day
Only one partner has his or her way

Expect more than just endearment
There won't always be agreement
Accept this in your life together
Just as you would stormy weather

Realize after mate selection
That you will not find perfection
Good marriages by loving spouses
Must be built like solid houses

Quarrels do not mean, "Of course
Let's now quickly get a divorce."
Both joys and quarrels come with sharing
Among people who are caring.

## 29.  WHAT FALSE RUMOR CHANGED THE FISH WORLD?

The herring said, "Say listen boys
What is all this confusion and noise?"
The flounder said, "It's all over town
There's a ship with people that's coming down."

The herring replied, "Oh gee, that's too bad,"
But in his heart he really was glad
The fish-folks always find it a pleasure
To go nosing about for human treasure

Plenty of ship wrecks is what they all wish
For what fish is to man, man is to fish

From every sea corner the fish people came
It reminded one of a World Series Game
Some fish were calm, but most were excited
A few were sullen but most were delighted

In honor of the event of the day
The old conventions were all thrown away
The shark said, "There is no need to be formal
For once in my life I'm going to act normal

And soon the dogfish began to meow
For years he had secretly studied how
The cat-fish joyously gave forth a bark
She had practiced it long, alone in the dark
Each fish was glad it now had permission
To be released from its inhibition

I'm sure that all people will think
It's good, in the storm, the ship didn't sink
After the captain had turned off the alarm
The fun the fish had did the people no harm

This proves that rumors don't have to be true
To create excitement and start something new
This story shows us that we all can have fun
By the kinds of events that don't hurt anyone.


## 30. A MOTHER'S VIEW OF WOMEN'S LIBERATION

At last, everything that men can do
Women have proven they can do too

To keep women removed from life's scene
Can only be called chauvinistic and mean

For centuries women were men's slaves
And have gone unfulfilled to their graves
We all know these restriction are bad
(But I still love my brothers and dad)

My mate knows I'm right and the logic behind it
I am sorry to say, he must still be reminded
But I think that at last he's seen the light
Because now he's less demanding at night

I've often wondered about chromosome Y
What's in it that makes men so brutish and why
It's hard to imagine my son as a brute
He's now so little, and loving and cute

I wonder if men have something interior
That tends to make them think they're superior
Anatomical differences are inescapable
But that doesn't make men any more capable

What's strange in all this is the well known fact
It's mothers who teach their sons how to act
Some have told them that it even could be
That our Father in Heaven is really a She

Let's not waste our time in such speculations
Which consists mostly of accusations
Lets agree instead that in a superior nation
We all should have equal self-actualization.

## 31.  MERRY-GO-ROUND

Did you ever hear of the old song
Of the dachshund who was so very long
That he believed when he turned around
The rear of a new dog he'd found?

He wished to meet this dog face to face
And looked for the creature every place
Judging from its back, the thing was a dear
But he wanted to see more than its rear!

One day he started to chase the beast
And he chased it for an hour at least
Exhausted he gave up at last
Amazed that this dog could run so fast.


## 32.  WILL IT RAIN?

She viewed the sky and tried to guess
How, with such dark clouds one should dress
She viewed the paper, read again
Those crisp, authoritative words, "It will not rain!"

Seldom in life, it's also rare in fiction
That one finds such a great contradiction
The dark sky clearly said, "Rain will be there"
The morning paper plainly said, "Warmer and fair."

"To be or not to be?" did Hamlet ask
His question was simple compared to her task
There was no way out of her despair
To rain or not to rain and what to wear?

She asked her dad who was a smart feller
He said, "My dear, carry an umbrella
Of life's great problems you needn't be scared
If you will face them adequately prepared."


## 33.   IN THE MORNING

Did you ever ride early in the morning
With the horses' heads turned towards the red of the
                                        sky
And notice as you took turns at cantering and galloping
That you owned the world, owned the whole world

Sharing it only with the splendid animal
That easily carries you along the shaded path
Through the silver green mists of unveiling nature
And the sweet damp smell of moist earth and grass?

Did you notice then how the wind
Fresh and carefree like a young living thing
Eagerly raced with you?
Its own winged steed invisible
Riding neck to neck with your black charger?

The wind's steed seemed to win then yours
And then the wind's again, and then together
You both  darted, laughing, into a wooded grove.


## 34.   ALONE BUT NOT LONELY

If you are alone and lonely
Split yourself into two
I don't mean become a dual personality
And certainly not schizophrenic
But become a friend to yourself

After you have met yourself
And introduced yourself to you, with a smile
You will find that you are in pleasant company
And no longer lonely, even when you are alone.


## 35.  ONLY AFTER WINTER GOES

Only after winter goes
Only after melted snows
Comes the warm awakening and
The soft murmurs on the land

Like a bud unfolds to leaf
Often time unwrinkles grief
As a flower springs from seed
Good things are the buds of need

Don't think that all hope is gone
And your future is forlorn
The sweet thought-flowers of tomorrow
Grow on stems of present sorrow.


## 36.  THE WORLD IS BETTER THAN YOU THINK

Murder and rape scream the headlines
Followed by yesterday's jailings and fines
Disgusted, you now turn to page two
For something more cheerful that's new

You read that another war has started
Then there's the list of the recent departed
Page three tells of a punk having fun
Shooting at people with an assault gun

On page four a banker confesses
He bilked a woman of all she possesses
And caused many heartaches, headaches and tears
By mishandling his clients' money for years

To keep their faithful readers subscribing
Newspapers report people wounded and dying
Show photos of abandoned kids crying
You fold up the paper, depressed and sighing

The news on the television is even worse
It shows a crime victim carried into a hearse
On the screen you see an old woman sobbing
She was a victim of a beating and robbing

The world is going to ruin you're sure
As every day you feel less secure
You hide when you hear a car come too near
A drive-by shooting is what you fear

One day you have to go to the store
Silently you sneak through the door
Carefully you look all around
Trying hard not to make any sound

You see no one who looks suspicious
Nor meet anyone who is vicious
There are no blood stains under your feet
You see no corpses lying on the street

Instead, you see little children at play
One of them says, "Have a good day!"
A couple approaches walking arm in arm
They walk right past you and do you no harm

When later you arrive at the store
Someone leaving holds open the door
You expect him to hit you or even worse
Demand at gun point that you give him your purse

After watching television last night
How could you have known he was merely polite
In the store you are surprised to find
The people you see there are friendly and kind

Encouraged by this you go to the mall
When there, you encounter no robbers at all
There are only nice people, dads and mothers
Young people, old people, talking to others

With your faith in humanity now restored
You buy some things you can afford
No longer are you frightened and sad
When you realize that not all people are bad

Now, when you read the paper or watch TV
You know in advance only bad people you'll see
Good people seldom make any news
To the media they're of no earthly use!


## 37.  SOLACE AT NIGHT

The sun is gone
The hills are dark
The moon smiles down
Upon the earth

Pretend tonight
You have no woes
Imagine that
You have no foes

Now close your eyes
Let peace descend
Sleep peacefully
God is your friend.


## 38.   HOME SWEET HOME

A turtle boasted to a mouse
"Wherever I go I carry my house
But you must hither and thither roam
Before you find yourself a home."

The mouse who was quite dignified
With a disdainful look replied
"I'm very happy that I lack
Your heavy burden on my back."

"I'm better off," the turtle said
"If someone whacked us on our head
And kept it up you'd soon be dead
While I would safely be in bed."

"Wrong!" said the mouse, "I'd find a hole
And save myself, body and soul
While you beneath your ugly shell
Would soon be crushed and go to hell!"

A worm nearby heard their dispute
He thought himself as quite astute

"The mouse is right!" he arbitrated
This made the turtle irritated

Just then came a torrential rain
The mouse searched for a hole in vain
The rain turned into icy hail
The worm wished he'd been born a snail

The mouse was shivering and scared
"I've changed my mind," the worm declared
"The turtle really is the winner
I'd share his shell if I were thinner."

Now here's the lesson of this poem
Appreciate your home sweet home
When it rains hard, stay in your house
And don't share it with any mouse.


## 39.  STILL ALIVE

Cut your finger with a knife?
Had a battle with your wife?
Shrubs you planted failed to thrive?
Just be glad you're still alive

Got yourself stung by a bee?
Drove your car into a tree?
Now have bruises on your knee?
Just be glad you're still alive

Boss told you that you're fired?
And that makes you sick and tired
Angry, sad and uninspired
Sorry now to be alive?

Take life as it comes instead
Not much happens when you're dead
I'll repeat what I have said
Just be glad that you're alive!

If good luck should come tomorrow
Gone would be your sighs and sorrow
But for good luck to arrive
You'd still have to be alive!


## 40.  ASK YOUR HEART

I'll say this right from the start
Nothings that's not from the heart
Even the most ardent kiss
Fails to bring much joy or bliss
One can kiss and stay apart
If it doesn't come from the heart

Don't believe all that appears
Whether laughter, smiles nor tears
Neither praise nor flattery
Always are what they seem to be
In true love, words play no part
Unless they come from the heart

Many things said are not real
They don't change the way you feel
Many praises that you hear
Were designed to catch your ear
For your heart they were not meant
From the heart they were not sent

Some gifts wrapped in fancy ribbons
Are only out of duty given

According to a certain date
Or merely to commemorate
A chronological event
From the heart they were not sent

Sometimes loving words are spoken
That serve only as a token
Kind some are, but you have seen it
That they really didn't mean it
From true love keep these apart
How to do it?  Ask your heart.


## 41.  A PLEASANT THOUGHT

Look up at the sky
Even if it is raining
And all you can see is clouds
Somewhere above these, there's is a blue sky

Look back on your life
Even if things aren't going right
And you are disappointed
Somewhere within you, there's a pleasant thought

Your dreams have not come true
Your hopes have not been fulfilled
And you are upset by troubles
Push these aside for just a moment

And search for a pleasant thought
You can find one waiting somewhere
If you decide to look hard for it
And to welcome it after you find it

Add to your tears and sighs
Just one little, pleasant thought
Then, like a rainbow among clouds
Watch the world change.


## 42.  OUR MIRROR

We need people because they are the mirror
In which we find our image
No matter how people differ from us
Their difference and likeness tell us who we are

Without people we do not really exist
We don't need them just to help us
Nor do we need them only for closeness
Of course we need them for both of these

But beyond that
We need people to gain an identity
We exists within them as well as within ourselves
Without them we cease to be

Hermits living in isolation do not know
That secretly in their minds
The people from whom they withdrew
Live within them and converse with them

No one can exist without people
Both our friends and foes reveal
Who we really are and where in our life
We came from and are going.

## 43.  JOE'S TREE

Joe was my friend and now I think of him
As I look at the tree he planted
He helped me when I needed him
To do tasks around the house I could not do alone

He was younger and stronger than I
Sometimes I'd see him across the street
Spreading bread crumbs for the waiting birds
He had a heart of gold, smiling, friendly, caring

Seldom have I ever known a nicer person
I was lucky to have him as my neighbor
And then cancer came to visit him
It was the virulent, hopeless kind

He fought it, took therapies, suffered through them,
Struggled with their side effects
Watching him was sad
He accepted it, complaining, yet still smiled at times

He fought on with tears behind his eyes
Then, at last, the time had come for resignation
He knew he must let go
He had fought a good battle, now he had to leave

He had lived a good life
We regretted that he had to die so young
He had been strong and vigorous
Until cancer paid him a visit and took him along

He was buried in the veteran's cemetery
He had fought for the United States
He had given of himself to his country
And to his neighbors and especially to me

His wife moved out of the house next door
She sold it to someone else
And with that its soul left it
Its blank windows now stared into space

The new neighbors were not friendly
There was a gap in my life and bitterness
Joe was gone, so good, so young, so permanently
And then, one day as I sat on my doorstep

I glanced at the house where Joe had lived
My eyes turned to the tree Joe planted
It was near the line that divided our properties
I was there when he had put it into the ground

It was a small tree then, young, tender, a child
It was much larger now, it had grown into a young adult
Suddenly it seemed as if Joe had come back
And was smiling, looking at his tree

My eyes turned to his small garden
He had placed some bushes over there
The flowers he had planted near the entrance
Now were in full bloom

The house appeared friendly again
The windows no longer stared vacantly
Somehow Joe had come back home
And made everything all right

Perhaps, it was that Joe had never left
The tree he had planted, all the things he had done
Remained  here, in that way Joe also remained
Still living in my memory as my good friend

There is more kindness, more caring,
More goodness, because Joe had lived
Goodness does not disappear, nor does kindness
Death does not undo them

Whatever happens remains eternal
Even cancer cannot take away the past
Nothing can erase goodness and love
Yes, Joe lives on.


## 44.  EXULTATION

In the warmth of the unknown
In the glow of it
In the darkness and the silence
There is a song, there is a light

There is giddiness
There is exultation
In the groping
In the fingertips alive
Poised for the touch of something

There is wild joy
In the anticipation of a sound
In the stillness

There is wonder, there is awe
In expectation of something
In the heart of nothingness

Yes, nothingness has a heart
Just as you and I have
And what counts most is
There is something in it.

## 45.  FRAGMENTS

When I found the small corner of paper money
On the floor of a city Post Office
I realized that it was not negotiable
Since it was only a fragment of something bigger

So is it with knowledge and truth
The value of what we learn depends
Not only on its genuineness but also
On whether it reflects the whole picture

If we explore only a fragment of knowledge
And assume that we have discovered
All the knowledge we need for living
We shall find that what we have gained
Is not negotiable.


## 46.  HOW A SARDINE BECAME THE KING

All the sea's fishes stood in a ring
To choose someone to be their king
The sea-lion growled, "I understand
That lions rule up on the land!"

The swordfish said, "Well, that may be
But you're not on land, you're in the sea
Besides, they say in the land of men
That the sword is mightier than the pen."

"You have that wrong!" the sea-lion roared
"The pen is mightier than the sword!"
The shark then spoke, "To tell the truth
Not pen nor sword but it is tooth!"

"Perhaps," chortled the jolly whale
"But size counts when those others fail."
"Not so," piped up the long, thin eel
"It's speed that counts, isn't it, seal?"

The shark then said, "I've an idea
Let's fight it out right now and here
And he who's left to tell the tale
Will be our king, it cannot fail!"

They all agreed.  The waters boiled
As tooth and fin in combat toiled
The air was filled with moans and sighing
The water filled with dead and dying

Soon all were dead save the sardine
Who by the rest had not been seen
Because he was so weak and small
And now he is king over all.*

--------

* Could this apply to our own future some day?


## 47.  DOING GOOD VERSUS DO-GOODERS

There is a difference
Between do-gooders and people who do good
Do-gooders do good to feel better about themselves
That is why their causes are often irrelevant
Impulsive and poorly thought out

They are concerned about their self-image
And expect applause because they need it
They have convinced themselves
That being a do-gooder is doing good

People who really do good don't need applause
They want us to live in a better world
They do not congratulate themselves
Self-righteousness is alien to them

If you can't really do good, my friend
Don't become a do-gooder
You would only be wasting your time
And get in the way of people who do good.


## 48.  THE BEAUTY CONTEST THAT WASN'T

"I've called a meeting to suggest
That we have a beauty contest."
It was the tall giraffe who spoke
The others thought it was a joke

He said, "I'm sure that I shall win
Because I am so tall and thin
I'm handsome," he went on to say
"Because I was born that way."

The others thought it might be fun
And now the contest had begun -
"With your long neck and legs, Giraffe,
Just looking at you makes us laugh!"

The elephant said "you can see
My beauty when you look at me

My shapely trunk and floppy ears
Deserve your vote and all your cheers."

The lion growled, "What you call 'trunk,'
Is nothing but a lot of bunk
It's not a trunk as you suppose
It's just a long and ugly nose!

Instead, look at my lordly mane
It makes comparisons in vain
I'm king of beasts as you should know
And I will win the beauty show!"

The deer said, "Lion, don't come near
You don't look handsome to a deer
Your royalty doesn't impress me
I believe in democracy!"

"There's no one else who has been born
Can match the beauty of my horn
Why don't you all just give up hope,"
Proudly declared the antelope

The pig whose middle was a tub
Had joined a fat-is-beautiful club
He oinked, "Our membership has found
Beauty increases with each pound."

As they quarreled, an alligator
Left his river and said later,
"My gorgeous teeth are beauty's treasure
I use them with a lot of pleasure."

"Not true," then hissed a curled-up snake
"All of your beauty claims are fake

Nothing destroys a body's charms
As much as having legs and arms."

The rhino said, "I take great pride
In my lone horn and my tough hide."
With little chance to win, the goats
Pinned all their hopes on absentee votes.

The zebra said, "It's what you eat
I earned my stripes by skipping meat."
"I'm better looking," claimed the fox
"From dining on bagels and lox."

The kangaroo said, "In my pouch
My baby makes me say, ouch, ouch!"
An ape sneered, "Just because you're dutiful
Does not mean that you are beautiful!"

I win the contest," shouted the ape
"Because of my near-human shape."
"We disagree, the humans fake it,
By hiding themselves when they're naked."

On this all animals agreed
And changed the contest with great speed
From most beautiful to ugliest
They liked this kind of contest best

It took no speeches to decide
That humans have something to hide
They voted humans short or tall
By far were ugliest of all

Most arguments can be resolved
When one's own pride is not involved
Choosing the ugliest to envision
Quickly avoids all competition.

## 49. WHAT IS TRUE LOVE?

What is true love?
The answer may surprise you
It is not the never-can-be heaven
Of unfulfilled dreams
More than anything else it is self-discovery
Through the mirror of another person

Only when you live in close contact
With someone else
Can you discover who you really are
After that discovery be prepared
Not always to like what you see

Many have been misled
By their false fantasies of love
True love's ingredients are dedication
Patience, loyalty and inevitable pangs of guilt

True love consists of more
Than just precious shared memories
It consists also of deliberate forgetting
Love brings pain and tears
As well as smiles and laughter
And if the love is true
The tears count most of all

When people talk of love
As two becoming one
They are mistaken
Such love falls apart
In the first storm of the season

Instead, if you love someone
There will be four of you instead of two
Only two of the four can love intensely
The other two remain behind closed doors

Is love togetherness?
Yes, up to a point
But true love also takes solitary trips
Into the past and future
Which each lover travels alone

True love permits the kind of sharing
That accepts another's not sharing
True lovers may inhabit different worlds
While clasping hands

True love is not a bag of jewels
It is a bag of mixed emotions
In which one pushes this and that aside
Until one finds hidden deep within it
Life's greatest joy.


## 50.   COMPUTERS VERSUS HUMANS*

Humans aren't computers
Humans aren't machines
Computers require chips
Humans need genes

Humans can make computers
There's much that these can do
Humans can make robots
But only God can make you.

———————

* This brings up-to-date Joyce Kilmer's (American poet,
1886 -1918) famous lines:
"Poems are made by fools like me,
But only God can make a tree."


## 51.  UNNECESSARY  REGRET

We live our lives with regret
Because we can never forget
That what we did was no good
Though we did the best we could

The problem is we neglect
To realize in retrospect
That the focus isn't on "should"
If we did the best could

It's true we'd do better now
That we've learned the why and how
To blame us in retrospect
Changes nothing and has no effect

I'm not talking here of crime
Just little things that with time
Make us think that we're no good
Though we did the best we could

It's senseless to reprimand
Someone who can't understand
That no woman nor any man
Can do more than the best they can

Let's stop regretting our past
And come to realize at last
That if our intentions were good
We did the best we could.


## 52.  MOSQUITO BITES

There are many insects that torture man
The mosquito is the worst of his clan
True, bees can give one a vicious sting
But mosquitoes seem to thrive on the thing

There are many dishes mosquitoes could eat
Without disturbing a pair of bare feet
And just to add insult to all this wrong
They hum all the while their bloodthirsty song

If people, instead of arming to fight
Would all take up spray-cans and unite
To put the pesky mosquito to rout
And make the world safe for the camper-out
Then many of us would thank the Lord
Our faith in humanity would be restored.


## 53.  NEW VISTAS

Sorrow from what happened to you
Stirs within you and will not let you rest
"Why has it happened to me?" you ask
"How cruel, how undeserved it is!"

Don't run away from your sorrow
Take a long, lingering look at it
To show it you have the courage to face it
Only, thereafter, will it not pursue you

Then you may turn your head away from sorrow
And lift your eyes above the darkness
Open them wide enough to see
Hope waiting for you to find it

Hope will bring with it sunlight
That you never thought you'd see again
Hope will reveal new vistas
That you never thought were there

The world is larger than you think
There is more in it than sorrow
There is more in your life than today
A fading of a flower heralds a new bloom

Make room in your mind for hope
Open wide the door to welcome it
And you may be surprised to see
Sorrow sneaking out of the open door.


## 54.   SELF-HATE

If you hate yourself you cannot love others
Because you see yourselves in them
In order to love yourself
You must accept yourself first, and if you do
It will change the way you live and think

Forgive yourself so that you can forgive others
The Golden Rule applies to us in the reverse
Treat yourself as you wish others would treat you
You can then love others and they will return your love

Self-hate comes to all of those who yearn
To leave their footprints on the sands of time
And don't take into account that winds will come
And blow upon on them and sweep them away.


## 55.  DEATH HAS TAKEN SOMEONE YOU LOVE

Death has taken someone you love
Be glad that your loved one does not share your grief
For those who leave us there is only peace
You are the one deprived – not your loved one
There is comfort in this

Life always is the winner over death
Death steals away life but cannot destroy it
Even if life lasts but for a brief moment
It has changed the universe by existing
The world will never be the same as it was before

Within your grief be glad
That your loved one has warmed your heart
And that this warmth is eternal
Because it has become a building block
Of all of that of which the world is made

Therefore, think of what was
And not of what could have been
What "was" existed
What "could have been" did not
Only for the dead are these the same

Death is a reunion with the infinite
All of us will meet it bearing gifts
No one leaves life empty-handed
The kind of life we lived is our gift to the infinite
And, believe it or not, it says, "thanks."


## 56.   A FROG'S JUMP

A spider to a frog said, "Why
Don't you be more like me?
Give up your silly jumping, try
To spin a web to catch the fly
It's better, don't you see?"

The frog croaked, "Yes, it is a sin
To jump as I must do
When all *you* need to do is spin
And wait for flies to wander in
To make your dreams come true."

"But," said the frog and jumped and caught
The spider in it's jaws
"There's something that you really ought
To learn from me because
He who like me can jump up high
Gets both the spider *and* the fly!"


## 57.   YOU CAN'T GET WHAT'S NOT THERE

If your need for milk is great
For a cow you'll have to wait

You can't get milk from a bull
No matter what on him you pull
You can't get water from a stone
You can't get steaks from a bone
You can't get love, as long as you live
From someone who has none to give.


## 58.  AN OYSTER RUMINATES

An oyster sat alone
Upon a slab of stone
At the bottom of the sea
And very sad was he

It was his fervent wish
To be like other fish
Who swim and dive and roam
Through water, wave, and foam

He said, "The truth to tell
My trouble is my shell
For there will only fit
I, myself, into it

What fun is there to be
Always inside with me?
It would thrill me with pride
To welcome friends inside."


## 59.  HEROES

The world does not lack heroes
People fail to recognize them
We don't know where to look for them
We think heroes are always applauded
When, in truth, heroism is often silent and invisible

We have heroes who have fought our wars
There are heroes who saved people's lives
But we also have other kinds of heroes
Who fought battles against themselves
And conquered their fears and temptations

We have heroes who are true to their ideals
In the face of threats and ridicule
These heroes are willing to face disapproval
And say, "No!" to their peers
Who offer them friendship with strings attached

Alcoholics who stop drinking are heroes
The addicted who conquer their craving are heroes
And so are people who turn away from crime
Those who experience prejudice are heroes
If they are not prejudiced in return

There are heroes in hospitals and wheelchairs
There is no lack of heroes all around us
There is only the lack of teaching our young people
How to recognize those heroes who are not applauded
And how to become heroes themselves.


## 60.  IMAGINARY HURTS

Don't defend yourself
Against imaginary hurts
Don't fight battles
In wars that don't exist

Your life can become
One of strife and resentment
A sad  battlefield
Of your own making

Don't erect fences
To keep out attackers
Who are not there
Except in your own mind

Don't wear an armor
To ward off arrows
Aimed at your heart
Only in your imagination

All this is keeping you
From seeing that the world
Is really beautiful
And that you are a fool.


## 61.   A FUNNY LOOKING DOG

I once had a dog
Wumpoo was his name
Happily he wagged his tail
Whenever I came
"Wumpoo," I used to say
"Believe me, it's true
Had I a tail to wag
I would wag mine too!"

Wumpoo was part airedale
The rest was poodle and chow
How did they get into one?
I'm sure I don't know how
But grown-ups used to smile and say
Lots of dogs had a share
To account for Wumpoo's looks
His paws, his face and hair

It didn't used to bother me
I didn't care at all
As long as Wumpoo came to me
Whenever I gave his call
No matter what his pedigree
Or from what ancestors he came
I knew there was a loving heart
Inside his funny frame.


## 62.   WHEN GUESSING IS A BLESSING

The challenge of living
Isn't taking or giving
Nor is it possessing
It's guessing!

Without contradiction
Neither fact nor fiction
Can reveal the real you
Like your guesses do

Whenever you mask
Your true self and ask
"Who am I?"  It's a blessing
You're just guessing.


## 63.   A MOST UNUSUAL SHARK

"My dear flounder," said the shark
Underneath the waters dark
"You seem vexed by many troubles!"
And the flounder thus replied
"I have tried and tried and tried
Yet I can't succeed in blowing any bubbles!"
Said the shark, "I surely will

Cure you of this little ill
Swim here closer, come and watch me do it
Blow like this and while you float
Twist your tongue back in your throat
Swim here closer if you wish to view it!"

Said the flounder, "You are kind
Fish like you are hard to find
You are that rare fish they call 'unselfish'
But although I'd gladly know
How I could some bubble blow
I prefer to take my lessons from a shellfish!"


## 64.  PLEASE FEEL SORRY FOR YOURSELF

They say you shouldn't feel sorry for yourself
Please do so, because self-pity
Is a sweet sorrow
Like a warm bath it soothes you

Self-pity is a delightful sadness
It is self meeting self
It is you, caring and nurturing yourself
It is you, mothering yourself

If you feel sorry for yourself
You are never alone
You have become your own companion
Take a moment and feel sorry for yourself
And as you do a miracle may happen

From the depth of your self-pity
A veil will lift, and behind it
You will see a smiling face
You will recognize it immediately
It is yours

They say, "Don't feel sorry for yourself"
But they are wrong.  Behind self-pity
There is love
Love is good for all of us
No matter where it comes from
Even if it's from you to you

The mistake those make
Who say, "Don't feel sorry for yourself"
Is that they forget
That what you should not do
Is to deny that you feel sorry for yourself

The veil will never lift
And you may succumb to despair
If you don't admit
That you feel sorry for yourself

If you're not intimidated
By those who say it's wrong
Self pity is sweet candy without calories
It is like a spring rain
That leaves you refreshed and renewed

So please feel sorry for yourself
If your self-pity is deserved
Enjoy it, and it's stay will not be long
And will not become your way of life.


## 65.   THOSE WHO SUFFER

Why are those who suffer
God's favorite children?
Because they alone have tasted
The deep, bitter earth
That is part of His universe

In their sorrow and suffering
They have discovered a secret
It is that meaning in life
Lies far beneath shallow happiness

Even if they are unaware of it
Those who suffer, experience
The ultimate dimension
Of life's preciousness

Tears of joy and tears of pain
Express extremes of emotions
That are closer to each other
Than the barren middle ground

The valleys and the mountains
The sky and the earth
The heights and the lows of life
Give each other their identity

Some say, "Rid yourself of sorrow
Escape from it as fast as possible
Do anything that you can
To live in a paradise that is unreal!"

If you do so, you will shed your sorrow
And in your blindness
You will stumble through life
Feeling happy.


## 66.  CONSOLATION

It's not how long people live
It's how much they live that matters
Long life is only a blessing
When it's a good life too

But what is a good life?
That's just what many don't know
A good life is your own life
At this very moment

You shake your head in protest
"I have too many problems
Too many things have gone wrong
My life is a tragedy!" you say

True, you don't have a good life
Because you see only your tragedy
You see only life's weeds
And not its flowers

Life can be very sad
But it can be also be good
Even if you have many problems

You are drowning in sorrow
Because you've stopped swimming
Take a deep breath now
And open your eyes

Let them sweep over the horizon
And search for a future
Where, though pain remains
Good things still are within reach.

## 67.  LUCY'S "GREAT WALL OF CHINA"

Early each morning
Lucy took her daily walk
Along a street near her home

Every day on her walk
She passed a view of great beauty
A valley ringed with trees and hills

As she walked back home
She again passed this view
And its beauty lifted her spirit

One day a large sign announced
That a construction company
Would build luxury homes

In the fields that had nurtured
The bushes and the wild flowers
Where rabbits played and birds sang

Soon mechanized monsters arrived
That dug up the ground
And leveled the earth

When Lucy walked past her view
She saw men constructing
A gray wall of large cement blocks

Every morning the wall rose higher
Until the view disappeared
And the wall replaced it

The beautiful view shared by all
Now belonged only to those
Who would live behind the wall

As she walked past it one day
Lucy recalled a picture she had seen
Of the Great Wall of China

Built long ago to keep out raiding nomads
Who came from the North
And stole the people's treasures

Lucy thought, those who had built the wall
And had taken away her view
Were like the raiding nomads

One morning it occurred to Lucy
That the "Great Wall of China"
Had also taken a treasure

Away from those inside of it
Who now had the beautiful view
Exclusively for themselves

It was the privilege of sharing it
With those who had walked past it
And found their spirit lifted by its beauty

Lucy asked herself, who had lost more
Those who were deprived of the view
Or those who had deprived others of it?

———————

* The photos are of the view and of the actual wall that
later blocked it.  The wall and the view are real.  Lucy is
an imaginary person.

## 68.   HE ASKED FOR ADVICE*

I ask you Dr. Kent
Are you from heaven sent
To help me live my life
So I can love my wife
Who nags me night and day
Until I stay away?

I do sincerely hope
You'll tell me how to cope
With a boss who's a jerk
And complains about my work
How can I do some thinking
Instead of only drinking?

The truth is, I'll confess
My life is a big mess!
I had a drunken dad
All he did was get mad
My mom was fat and lazy
My sister wild and crazy

My brothers are in jail
No wonder that I fail!
My life consists of fears
Compulsions, booze and tears
Must I go down in shame?
If so, who is to blame?

P.S. My heart is filled with hate
Dear Shrink,  Is it too late?

(Dr. Kent's answer)

Dear hating suffering friend
Your broken life can mend

If, as you do your crying
You also do some trying!
I don't think it's too late
To make up with your mate

You might surprise the "jerk"
By doing better work
I don't care who's to blame
The fact remains the same
You're sure to go on losing
As long as you are boozing!

Get hate out of your heart
And then make a new start!

P.S.  Not only Dr. Kent,
We're *all* from heaven sent.

———————

* This verse appeared in my book, <u>A Psychologist</u>
<u>Answers Your Questions</u>, Dorrance & Co. 1987.  It was
used just to add a light touch to otherwise serious advice
and I reprinted here for the same reason.

## 69.   WHEN YOU'RE SULKING PRESS NUMBER FIVE

There was a time when in our nation
You wished to get some information
You dialed a number night or day
And heard a friendly voice say
"Don't worry, sir, I will connect you
So you can get your message through."
And you knew then even without seeing
That you were talking to a human being

Now when you try it, a recorded voice
Answers the phone and gives you this choice:
"If you want service just press number one,"
However, your troubles have just begun
In advance you know what's ahead for you
"If you want information press number two."

Whatever the next message may be
You're sure it will say "Now press number three."
And then if you want to hear any more
You know it already, "Press number four."
There's no doubt what's next to arrive,
"If you wish to start over press number five."

You feel abandoned and quite alone
And sadly cuddle your telephone
You are no wiser than you were before
So you have to dial the number once more
You get no answer but hear music played
You know what that means, your call is delayed

You wait and wait but no one is there
You hold the phone while you sit in your chair
The next time you call the line is busy
Slowly but surely you're getting dizzy
And now you're also somewhat thinner
Because of your phone call you missed your dinner

In spite of all your trouble and pain
Your total experience wasn't in vain
You gained a much greater appreciation
Of humans who give you information
Whenever you're sulking just press number five
And you'll welcome *anyone* who's alive.

# 70. OLD AGE'S COMPENSATION

If we live long enough we shall all reach a stage
Where we exchange our youth for old age
Throughout our lives on our birthday
We gain something new as our youth goes away

It's true, now we forget dates and all that
Where we left our glasses, our keys and our hat
We no longer can jog or run quite as fast
Nor play football and baseball as we did in the past

But we have sweet memories of long, long ago
They're priceless treasures that youth cannot know
This great blessing no young people can share
For the simple reason, they never were there

We forget what we say in our conversations
But old age still has its own compensations
Unlike, when young, we don't have to worry
Because in old age we're not in a hurry

It took some hard knocks and long years 'till we knew
If you can't change the world, *don't let it change you*
No need to consult any book on a shelf
We've learned life's secret, be true to yourself
Don't fret about your aches and your pains
Think of your memories and of your gains

You couldn't do much when you first got a start
But when you're old you did more than your part
Your reward is – even if you're hobbling around –
With trial and error, some wisdom you've found.

## 71.  APPRECIATION

Regardless of the effort you've spent
You still have to try to be content
If in your life you're so situated
That you are not appreciated

Sometimes the rewards you're due
Others will take away from you
In your life you may never receive
Credit for the things you achieve

You know it's unfair but try to ignore it
And in your memory do not store it
You didn't lose anything you had before
Those who ignored you lost much more.


## 72.  NOISE BELOW

Unearthly howls rose from the sea
I dove deep through the waves to see
What it could be

I saw about a hundred fish
Of all assortments one could wish
Playing a symphony

Using a sword instead of a hand
The swordfish led the finny band
With much emotion

And all the other fish-faced gents
Played loudly on their instruments
Down in the ocean

The whale he played the tuba deep
Enough to rouse the drowned from sleep
To hold their ears

The sardine played a fife so shrill
The dead aroused, again he'd kill
Amid their tears

The tuna-fish at the bassoon
Was always playing out of tune
It is a shame

Some like the things they haven't got
And put the very thing they're not
Into their name

With a mouth-organ in each arm
The octopus displayed his charm
To all the crowd

The turtle played upon the harp
His shell was flat his notes were sharp
And he played loud

The shark behind his music books
Gave the sea-lion dirty looks
He played trombone

The sea-lion who turned around
To scowl at the loud trombone's sound
Played saxophone

He said, "Oh shark when you begin
You spoil our music with your din
Stop! Rest! Relax!"

The shark replied, "*You* spoil our band
By making sounds no fish can stand
With that darned sax!"

The two blew louder than before
Well folks, it was an awful roar
And it got ever louder

An angry clam said, "Ah perhaps
We could make those two noisy chaps
Into clam chowder"

The rest swam off in great disgust
The two played on as if they'd bust
I saw them frown

Each tried to drown the other out
One fact they had forgotten about
Fish do not drown

The sun had set, the sea was dark
The tired sea-lion and shark
Were turning pale

On ships sailors made tight their ropes
And peered around through telescopes
For signs of gale

When all the fish returned to seek
The two, they found them very weak
To compensate them

The fish judged them detestable
Because they'd spoiled their festival
And then they ate them

If you play any instrument
Much time and effort you have spent
You can be proud

Get fun and pleasure out of it
I'll say this for your benefit
Don't play too loud!


## 73.   HOW TO ENJOY YOUR FUTURE

Behind the picture that you now are looking at
There is a larger picture which you do not see
Because you are staring too hard
At what you are looking at now

In your mind draw a circle
To stand for your life so far
Then within the circle draw a segment
That represents your present feelings

Even if your joy or sorrow is great
The segment in your circle
Does not encompass all of your life
Unless you drew it that way in error

In your imagination draw another circle
Let it stand for your future life
And divide it into large segments
That represent your hopes and dreams

Your hopes for the future may not be fulfilled
Your dreams for tomorrow may never come true
But just by wishing, dreaming and longing
You enlarged the segment you drew of today.

## 74.  AN INSIGHT

Since it was God's wish
To be the Father of a Son who was Jewish
It isn't at all odd
That a dislike of Jews reflects on God

The Bible says God sent
Jews to write the Old Testament
All of us need to understand
That's why He gave the Jews back their land

Now and then a false critic
Makes statements antisemitic
Condemning a people as a whole
For any single person's role

Fair-minded people are aware
That all the races have their share
Of people kind and people mean
With most of them in-between

Since God, Himself, created races
With different skins and different faces
Bigotry in any nation
Is against God, an accusation.


## 75.  "I'M RIGHT!"

Some people spend their day and night
Proving to others that they are right
They then declare all others wrong
And argue about it loud and long

What causes some people to argue and fight
To convince the whole world that they're right
About everything no matter how small
About things that don't matter at all?

Why must they try to prove others wrong
Continue to prove it and the subject prolong
Until those who listen can stand it no more
And run from the room and slam the door

Self-righteousness is a defect
That causes people to lose their respect
For those who seem to lack what it takes
To admit, like all of us, they make mistakes

The need they have to always be right
Can also be seen in a different light
Beneath it lies thinking, "I'm misunderstood"
And beneath that is the thought, "I'm no good!"


## 76.  THE JOY OF TRAVELING

Said an old traveler whom I once met
I haven't finished my traveling yet
There's hardly enough that I have seen
To satisfy my traveling gene

Whenever I hear of a distant shore
I'm am ready to see it and travel some more
And if I have never been there before
I can hardly wait to get out of my door

When I hear of foreign ladies and men
I get the urge to travel again

There's something strange about human faces
They look more exotic in distant places

I've found other travelers quite different from me
They come to look down on whatever they see
When they examine a foreign interior
It makes them feel that they're superior

There's no escape since I always must
Give in to my restless wanderlust
Neither hassles, nor pills, nor inoculations
Could ever deter me from foreign vacations

And all the delays and the baggage I lug
Could never kill off my traveling bug
I seldom feel as ecstatic and good
As when I leave my own neighborhood

But there's a catch, which I find confusing
It makes my travels just a bit less amusing
It's that no matter wherever I roam
I'm most inspired when I'm reminded of home

When I see a landscape, a cat, or a tree
Like one I could have stayed home to see
I give them a loving, nostalgic smile
And thank them for making my journey worthwhile.


## 77.   TO THE NEWLYWEDS*

We planned to give you for your wedding
Something you could use, like bedding
Something you could touch and see
Like a toaster or TV

Something which in future years
All your children and your peers
Would be told,  "This gift was sent
By our Mom and Daddy Kent!"

Money comes and money goes
Where it goes to no one knows
All we know is with the years
Money always disappears!

Money given doesn't show
No big package with a bow
Nothing that has large dimensions
Like the kind of gifts one mentions

Yet with love we both agreed
To give something that you need
It came to us in a flash
What our kids need now is *cash!*

---

* I wrote this verse to accompany the check we gave our
son and his wife as their wedding present from us.


## 78. A DISCOURAGED PERSON*

Like a naked tree
On a little hill
When sweet summer's gone
And the winds are chill

Like a drifting cloud
Near the pale round moon

That will blot its light
And obscure it soon

Like a feathered thrush
Frozen in the snow
Never more to sing
Its notes sweet and low

All nature reflects
Its frustrations here
In my saddened soul
And my bitter tear

You ask why I'm sad
Why is it I weep
Life is hard, not sweet
Death is death, not sleep.

———————

*The poem that follows could be a response to it.

## 79.  THE FRAGMENT AND THE WHOLE

Don't view a fragment of reality
As the whole of reality
For it will narrow your view
And make you unaware of life's meaning

If someone makes a mistake
The mistake is only a fragment of the person
Don't view the whole person as a mistake
For then you will become  one yourself

If you view only a fragment of the Big Picture
You will deprive your world of beauty and significance
And that will put achieving happiness
Out of your reach

If you cannot forgive another's error
It is because you are staring at the ground
And do not see the sky, the sun, the trees, the flowers
That give the world its beauty. (See page 82.)


## 80.  MEANING OF LIFE

There are those who look for the meaning of life
They look for it in the sky and deep within the earth
They search the universe for it
They call upon God to show it to them

And if they can not find it conveniently
They look for it under their rugs
Or rummage in drawers seldom opened
They fail to realize that their search is futile

No one will really find meaning in life
Because it is everywhere and in everything
And that makes it invisible and untouchable
At most, you can find some of its footprints

These you see when you give or get a kiss
When you laugh and cry with others or alone
When you love and hope, when you work and rest
Its footprints show you that meaning exists

All things give meaning to life
That is why no one will ever find meaning itself
There is too much of it to see
And too much of anything
Can never be seen or found.


## 81.  THE INDECISIVE CAPTAIN*

"Sailing, sailing, over the bounding main -
Down, down, down!
Oh, if it would only stay there
Up, up, up!
You're making me sea-sick!
Oh, please captain, let it stay there!"

"Steward, maid, waitress, garçon - anyone!
Please tell the captain to make up his mind
Either UP! or DOWN!!
If he doesn't stop bouncing the ship around
I'll never book a cruise on this line again!"

———————————

*Can you relate the silly verse above to the serious poem
that follows?


## 82.  AD REM, AD HOMINEM

Don't hate the unjust
Hate injustice
Don't fight those who are afflicted
Fight the disease
Bury evil and you will scoop up evil-doers
With the same shovel

"Rem" is the Latin for the thing itself
"Hominem" refers to the person
"Ad" means against

Direct anger ad rem
Otherwise you will always lose in the end
No matter how many battles you may win
Against the wrongs perpetrated on earth

To keep people from hurting each other
You must sometimes use ad hominem methods
But don't think that you can prevent wrong-doing
By ad hominem approaches to the world's problems

Our jails overflow because our ad hominem methods
Cannot alter conditions that require ad rem remedies
Always attack ad rem - the evil itself
Otherwise you are attacking only shadows

Ad rem conditions need more than punishment
They require a change of heart, a new life outlook
All those who hope to make tomorrow better than today
Must know the difference between ad hominem and ad
                                                    rem.


## 83.  DAYDREAMS

Never are your daydreams in vain
They are beautiful jewels of your brain
They shine bright and delight your soul
And they have their own mysterious goal

Some people say, "they're unreal
Daydreams are like air no one can feel
They are only fiction and never are facts
They are only thoughts and never are acts."

There's something these critics don't understand
Daydreams build castles out of raw sand
With daydreams God, who is forgiving and wise
Allows us to return briefly to paradise.


## 84.  SELF-RIGHTEOUSNESS

Spare the word, "should"
It does you no good
To use it in teaching
Or even in preaching

"Should" used to blame
Or still worse to shame
Is not really instructive
Nor very productive

Neither does "ought"
Tell us a lot
Except to say
"Do it *my way*"

Remember your view
Belongs only to you
Another view might
Be just as right

Don't always be sure
Or feel too secure
That only you know
The best way to go.

# 85.  A TROUT EXERCISES SELF-CONTROL

A trout once saw a worm
Wiggle, squiggle, and squirm
Upon a sharp, black hook
Near the edge of a rippling brook

And he swam all around it
And gave the worm a look
"To my fishy, wishy eyes
You're a piece of paradise!"

Said the trout about to munch
But suddenly he got a hunch!
There are more important things, thought he
Than matters such as lunch

There are such things in life
As children, home and wife
And I'm sure that it is true
That it's safer not to chew

The trout said to the worm
"My intentions are now firm
Not to risk taking a bite
If I did, I think I might

Have to squirm and squiggle too
And be eaten just like you."
Never again did the trout look
At snacks dangling from a hook.

## 86.  THINGS ARE ETERNAL*

You don't have to be famous
You just have to be you
Remember that recorded
Are all the things you do

All things are eternal
Nothing disappears
Your hopes, your deeds, your daydream
Your laughter and your tears

Your deepest thoughts and secrets
Through light-years will not fade
Because they are the building blocks
Of which the world is made.

---------

*This poem reflects ideas in Chapter Two in my book,
Mapping The Human Genome–Reality, Morality, And
Deity, University Press of America, 1995

# 87.  NATURE'S GEMS*

What is a flower
In a dotted field
Or a rose in a garden of roses?

Out on a gray ash heap
Or in molding garbage
A single, simple blossom
Is a heaven to an earth

What is a tree
In a tall forest of trees
Where shade covers shade
In thick, dark layers?

What is a stream
In a valley of streams
Sparkling, laughing
Running toward the ocean?

A bent tree in a desert
Alone, or in a grove of dry, gray trees
A muddy stream creeping
Over bare sand parched with heat
Those are the gems of nature's splendor:
A single flower, a bent tree, a muddy stream.

————————

*This poem is taken from a collection of poems I wrote
while I was an undergraduate in college.  The
illustrations depict the single flower and the bent tree.

## 88.  LIVE DAY BY DAY

You have troubles and much sorrow
Therefore, don't think of tomorrow
That won't make them go away
You must face them day by day

If there's much you have to fear
Or you think your end is near
Then throughout your earthly stay
Go on living day by day

Every lovely flower pales
Nature has its storms and gales
If life's storms now head your way
To survive, live day by day

Don't dwell on the awful things
That you think tomorrow brings
All attention you must pay
To live only for today

You don't need to give up hope
And with life you still can cope
If you don't let your mind stray
From this goal, live day by day.


## 89.  NO MYSTERY IN MORALITY

Isn't it a great pity
That in every town and city
Some spend an entire life
In anger and constant strife
To make other people to see
What they mean by morality?

There's nothing to argue about
No reason "I'm right" to shout
For dissent there is no need
Since everyone always agreed
Moral people don't hurt others
And treat them as sisters and brothers

From traditions written and oral
For ages we've known what's moral
It's to follow the Golden Rule
That we learned in Sunday School
Almost every one will agree
It's the crux of morality

It's so easily understood
That to help other people is good
To hurt other people is bad
Therefore, isn't it rather sad
That so much wasted time is spent
In an ongoing argument

About what "morality" means
And whether it is in our genes
Or which explanation is right
Causing us to argue and fight
When all of us agree with the fact
Of how a moral person should *act?*

## 90.   DESERVED PEACE

Even with all the turmoil in the world
You can find peace within yourself
If you, yourself, make peace within yourself
And do not permit the world's turmoil to disturb it

By gaining peace yourself
You add it to the peace remaining in the world
But first you must search deeply to see
If room for peace exists within you

Inner peace is not a prescribed medication
It is not for sale in any pharmacy
If you try to mix guilt and peace of mind
The side effects become intolerable

No road leads you from guilt to peace of mind
Guilt blocks the way that you must travel
Therefore, repair the damage that caused your guilt
Before you travel further on your road

And yet, guilt is a precious gift to humankind
It is a guiding light in the night's darkness
You would not find the hidden place of truth
If guilt did not cast the beam that illuminates it.


## 91.  THE ROCK ON YOUR BACK*

That first hard rock you didn't choose
A second rock is of no use
Don't get upset – ask with concern
"What from the first rock can I learn?"

A second rock will weigh you down
It'll cause you grief and make you frown
Whatever happened bad before
A second rock will make it more.

---

*There are two kinds of symbolic "rocks" we carry on our back. The first "rock" stands for an unpleasant event that occurred in our lives. The second rock represents annoyance and anger at the fact that it happened to us.

This verse is taken from my book:
<u>A Psychologist Answers Your Question</u>. (Dorrance, 1987)


## 92.  GREATER APPRECIATION

If a thing worthless today
That we're apt to throw away
Is dug up and reappears
In about a thousand years

Scientists will test and measure it
Museums will buy and treasure it
Crowds will come from near and far
Just to gaze at it with awe

Any beer can found intact
Will be called an artifact
Judged as gorgeous and sublime
All it really takes is time

When today's junk is discovered
And our old bones are recovered
Eons later they will be
Priceless archeology

Please appreciate yourself
Before you adorn a museum shelf
View yourself with more affection
And don't wait till resurrection.

# 93. WHEELCHAIR AND LIFE

An accident happened
Was it an illness?
Or, perhaps, the ravages of age
Your feet have become wheels
They no longer can walk
They are no longer yours

Like many others who are wheelchair-bound
You must adjust to a new life
But remember this,
Worse things could have happened to you
Worse things do happen to people
Every day, every hour, every minute

The world remains available for you to enjoy
For you are able to think and breathe
You can still love the world
Whether you are sitting or standing

At this moment the good things that are yours
May be hidden in the fog of your despair
Meet your fate with courage
And be mindful of the blessings
That remain for you to enjoy

In time your inconveniences
May drift away like clouds in the wind
And you will see the sun shine again
As you make peace with your new life.

## 94.  THE HUMAN MIND

Things seen in a store
Tempt us much more
Than the suits or dresses
That one possesses

It's really deplorable
Things are adorable
When priced too high
For us to buy

If wishes came true
Other wishes new
Would quickly race
To take their place

Dissatisfaction
Is a reaction
To wanting more
Than we had before

In time we know
As older we grow
That every new yearning
Is one way of learning

That satisfied wishes
Like gourmet dishes
Disappear fast
Neither can last.

# 95. LOOKING BACK OVER YOUR SHOULDER*

Unconditional love is not enough
Because such love is too nearsighted
To see deeply down within you
Understanding is love wearing glasses

Understanding is more important than love
If love is anesthesia, understanding is medicine
If love is a blinding light, understanding is a lantern
That lights the way and reveals what is beneath the
                                                    surface

People say, "love me!" and mean "understand me!"
Understanding is a higher form of love
That some people don't recognize as "love"
Because they don't understand, understanding

If both love and understanding enter your life
You are in paradise, not because you deserve to be
But because you hitched a ride that passed by there
More likely by chance than by plan

But don't expect to live in paradise forever
Some famous people have been expelled from Eden
Understanding does not come with a lifetime warranty
Self-understanding is more enduring but lonely

If you have gained self-understanding you'll admit
That you often look back over your shoulder
To see if someone is following you who wants
To love you unconditionally.

## 96.  PEARLS

The greatest lesson from the animal world
Comes not from the majestic lion
Nor from the lordly eagle soaring in the sky
People have admired these
For their nobility throughout ages
But they do not teach us
What the lowly oyster does
As it clings silently and humbly
To a rock in its ocean bed

The oyster teaches us
That with tolerance and patience
We can transform an enemy
Into a source of joy to the world
Layer by layer
The oyster donates parts of itself
To transform an intruding
Grain of sand or a parasite
Into a gem of lustrous beauty

Pearls were used to pay taxes
In China in 2000 BC.
In Persia, and later
In Europe, only nobility
Were permitted to wear pearls
In Indian mythology
Pearls were heavenly dew drops
That fell into the sea
And were caught by shell fish
During the period of the full moon

In Hebrew legends pearls
Were the teardrops of Eve

After she was banished from Eden
Until the 17th century
The innocent pearls
Were ground up for medicine
And sold to the wealthy

In all these uses and in legends
The pearl's true value was ignored
And people remained unaware
That the oyster teaches us by its example
That we can love our enemy
And make him a friend

Pearls are valued
According to perfection of sphere
Symmetrical drop, size, semi-translucence
Deep luster, and fine texture
But even without these advantages
Every pearl teaches us the same lesson,
Out of an initial irritation
You can make a pearl.


## 97.   CREATING

By creating we awaken
The dormant potentialities
That lie within the womb of the cosmos

Too often, you and I
Live only for the fickle applause
That those who create may receive

Applause contributes nothing
Except visibility to assure us
That we exist

Our demand for applause
Leads to competition and struggle
While creating brings beauty to the world

By seeking applause
We replace substance with the shadows
That we pursue in vain for satisfaction

If we confuse showing with doing
And if we make applause our goal
We will stumble and lose our way

Those who create only to gain approval
Sell their souls to the highest bidder
And become vanity's slaves

Then, only a new goal – to be creative
Without a hurrah from the crowd
Can set us free.


## 98. THERE IS A PURPOSE IN THE WORLD

Some people tell us that the world lacks purpose
"Life has evolved through blind chance," they say
Random mutations account for natural selection
Produced by adaptation to an ever changing earth

In their myopia they view "the selfish gene"
As the supreme monarch of all things alive
The single-minded monarch gives but this command
"Survive, increase, spread me across the earth."

Let us not believe that we know all there is
About purpose in the universe, but we can ask
"Could it be that with the advent of human life
The universe found purpose that some fail to see?"

Where is the scientific evidence for purpose?
It lies unrecognized within that very question
Purpose is found in our asking who we are
Where are we going and what we can accomplish?

With humankind a purpose for the world was born
To banish random chance and replace it with justice
And to rebel against the rule of selfish genes
To sing, and dance, to play, and to create beauty

The world lacks neither purpose nor great goals
Because through human life it has acquired them
All who deny that the universe lacks purpose
Forget our a role in making the world what it is.


## 99.  WHEN LOVE AND HATE GROW

Each new love and new hate is drawn
To other loves and hates already within us
To make just one big love and one big hate
Both of them obsessed with their own growth

Big hate, in time, needs to vents its passion
Like an angry, mindless mob searching
Irrationally, for some convenient target
Upon which to express its overflowing wrath

Big love has need to spread out
To share itself with people, the earth, the universe
Until it encompasses all things that are
And becomes one with them.

Big hate tears down, big love builds up
But remember that both big love and big hate

Once were only tiny loves and hates
That. initially, seemed to be insignificant

So, if you love only a little or hate only little
Be prepared for each of these to grow powerful
As they join others of their kind within yourself
And change the world for better or for worse.

---

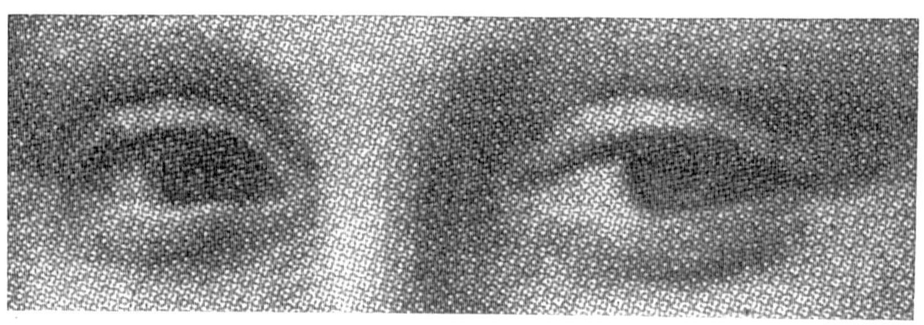

## 100.  THE RIDDLE OF A STRANGE ATTRACTION

Once long ago there was a woman
Who gave birth to a son in a cow-shed
The father of the child did not marry her
Because she lacked the wealth to suit his ambitions

The child's birth was kept secret
So that his mother could hide her identity
To give her an opportunity to marry
Someone who would accept her for herself

The boy was raised and nurtured by other women
And doted over by his father and grandfather
For his charm and unusual talents
But he was denied the education his father had

He grew into manhood and was restless
And looked for something that was lacking
He did not know where to find it or what it was
His life became an ongoing search for knowledge

His talents and his skills were admired
The rich and the powerful employed him
He did marvelous things for their pleasures
While his search for something undefinable continued

One night he dreamed he saw a woman
Her eyes were sad yet strangely vigilant
She seemed to ask him for protection
He felt himself respond to her hidden sorrow

The anguish in her eyes intrigued him
He knew at once, a women with such eyes
Smiles falsely to conceals something important
To gain acceptance in a world that broke her heart

The man who dreamt, woke up and thought
The woman in his dream resembled those
Who must perform on the broad stage of life
Our world demands pretense, our lives are make-
                              believes

Who was the woman in his dream wondered the man
A peasant girl?  A merchant's wife that he had met
Who suffered from her husband's stern demands?
Was it a soldier's widow? a model? a duchess?

Her high forehead was very much like his
Was it himself that he had sought – his inner soul?
Had he, at last, ended his frantic search?
His eyes filled with tears of real relief

Next night again he saw this woman in a dream
Her smile now was genuine and in her eyes shone love
She flung her arms around him and cried out, "my son!"
His search had ended as he whispered, "mother."

This man recalled that when he was a boy
No one would tell him who his mother was
Her secret must be kept, her sorrow masked
Like you and I, she smiled so that she could survive

His mind had created her from other women
To heal her wounds he now revealed them to the world
The multitudes that flocked to see her, saw themselves
Her wounds were theirs, and so was her pretending

In Italy they call her likeness La Gioconda
In France she is known as the La Joconde
The English-speaking world calls her the Mona Lisa
Leonardo's portrait sitters were but shadows
His mother filled the empty canvass of his heart.

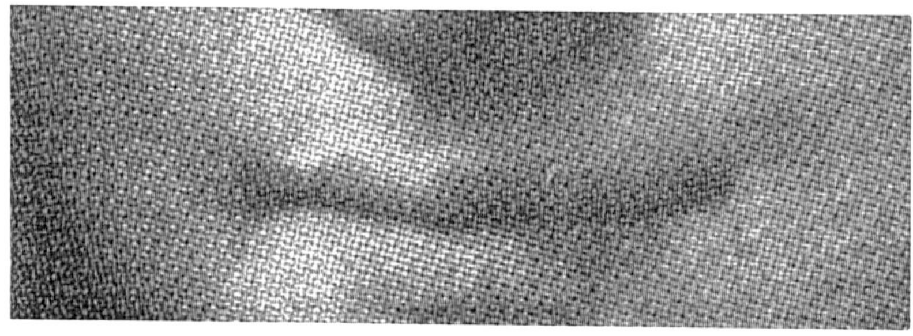

———————

# 101. THE LESSON A TREE TAUGHT ME*

*The Two Center Leaves*   (See front cover)

When most of us stop
To think about life
We glance backwards only
To the years of our youth (smaller center leaf)
Or forward only
To adulthood ahead (larger center leaf)
But to grasp its significance
We must view life's full sweep
From budding to decay (outer circle of leaves)


*The Circle of Leaves*

Then we know that life is
Strong, yet fragile
A feather drifting
Languidly in still air

Dancing in a wind
Convulsed in a storm's wrath
Always descending, inevitably
Towards the ground

Yet those inclined
May see death as a miracle
For death gives birth to life
And life gives birth to death

The leaf decays and falls
A gift to the soil
Nourishing and enriching it
Enabling the tree

To bear new buds
Which unfold
To live and die and live again.

———————

## *INSIDE OF FRONT AND BACK COVERS

The meaning of the leaves inside the front cover of this book can be found in the preceding verse. I gathered the leaves from my favorite tree, which always extended its arms towards me as I drove by it on my way to the Cocopah Indian Reservation.  Each Wednesday  I served the tribe as their psychologist.
One day a feather drifted down to earth from one of the branches where a bird had perched.  Inside the back cover of  this book (page 113) is a photograph I took of the actual tree.

# INDEX BY TITLE OF POEMS

———————